# Main Idea Maneuvers

Grades 1–3
L. D. Ceaser

Fearon Teacher Aids
a division of
**David S. Lake Publishers**
Belmont, California

*Editorial director:* Ina Tabibian
*Development editor:* Maureen E. Hay
*Managing editor:* Emily Hutchinson
*Production editor:* Stephen Feinstein
*Design director:* Eleanor Mennick
*Designer:* Colleen Forbes
*Illustrator:* Duane Bibby
*Compositor:* Pamela Cattich
*Manufacturing director:* Casimira Kostecki

ISBN 0-8224-1475-9

Printed in the United States of America
1. 9 8 7 6 5 4 3 2

# Contents

# Introduction

The lessons in this workbook develop the following eight subskills for determining main idea:

1. **Identifying Repetition and Redundancy**
2. **Determining Relevance**
3. **Classifying Nouns**
4. **Classifying Series of Events**
5. **Identifying Topic Sentences**
6. **Inventing Topic Sentences**
7. **Identifying Main Idea**
8. **Understanding and Using Titles**

At the conclusion of each activity is an evaluation code box.

| ○ = too easy | □ = too hard | △ = just right |
|---|---|---|

An evaluation of item difficulty can be made by enclosing the item number within one of the shapes shown in the box to relay the coded message. Another way to use the code box is simply to shade in the shape that best evaluates the page. This evaluation might be made by the teacher, the student, a tutor, or a team. The code is designed to help determine skill areas needing further attention.

The worksheets are organized by section, each section focusing on one of the eight subskills.

**1. Identifying Repetition and Redundancy**
This skill requires attention to vocabulary. In this section, the student notes antonyms, synonyms, and sentences with similar meaning.

**2. Determining Relevance**
In this section, the student seeks commonality among words in a list, illustrates words by drawing pictures, and identifies descriptive words and phrases.

**3. Classifying Nouns**
Identifying noun lists in sentences and categorizing objects under a superordinate term are essential skills for summary writing and finding main ideas. In this section, the student practices these skills.

**4. Classifying Series of Events**
Noticing sequential activities, determining common factors in activities, and finding subordinate and superordinate actions help the student understand the content. In this section, the student practices these skills.

### 5. Identifying Topic Sentences

A good topic sentence describes the purpose of the text material. In this section, the student finds topic sentences in short paragraphs.

### 6. Inventing Topic Sentences

The student who is able to originate a summary sentence demonstrates an understanding of main idea and establishes a deep comprehension of and memory for the material. In this section, the student invents topic sentences for lists and short paragraphs.

### 7. Identifying Main Idea

With an ability to recognize the main idea and appropriate supporting details of a reading selection, a student will be able to use print effectively as a learning tool. In this section, the student identifies main ideas and generates supporting details that are pertinent to specific topics.

### 8. Understanding and Using Titles

Effective use of titles provides clues to the organization of reading material and insights into its major concepts. In this section, the student creates titles for specified content and provides content pertinent to book titles.

Active reading, or deep processing of text material, enhances reading comprehension and helps the student apply new knowledge to life skills. The lessons in this workbook will improve language, writing, and thinking skills as they help the student fully experience the reading process. For this reason, oral discussion and a variety of responses are to be encouraged.

Summary writing skills may be applied to reading materials at all grade levels. While every passage will not contain all of the subskill elements covered in this text, applying the subskills often will help the student internalize the total summary writing strategy, thereby improving reading comprehension.

The following section suggests additional activities for continued practice in the subskills necessary for identifying main ideas and in understanding and using titles.

## Additional Activities

### 1. Classifying

Help students categorize nouns and verbs. Have them play "Twenty Questions" with categories. Here are some examples of categories you might wish to use:

| | |
|---|---|
| kinds of weather | temperature words |
| types of homes | names of games |
| names of colors | television shows |
| ways to feel | titles of books |
| types of dogs | location words |
| names of tools | types of food |
| classroom tools | names of cars |

Follow this procedure for "Twenty Questions":

- Choose a student to be "It."
- Have "It" think of an item in any category and say, for example, "I am thinking of a title."
- Have other students, in turn, ask questions that can be answered "Yes" or "No."
- The winner is the person who can guess the item before twenty "No" answers have been given.
- The winner can be the next "It." If no one guesses the item, the original "It" can go again.

### 2. Vocabulary

Vocabulary activities provide useful practice in thinking and deciding which are parts of the process of determining main ideas. Crossword puzzles, activities using synonyms and homonyms, and root word lessons are all beneficial. For example, have students try to make new words by using known prefixes and suffixes.

| | |
|---|---|
| dis- (opposite) | -able (able) |
| un- (not) | -ing (in process) |
| in- (not) | -s (plural) |
| re- (again) | -ed (past) |
| non- (none) | -est (most) |

### 3. Scrambled Words

Write scrambled words on the board. Tell students the category the words are in, and ask them to unscramble the words. Here are some examples:

> oatts, pplae, nnaaba: things we eat
> (toast, apple, banana)
>
> nur, kwal, pjmu: ways we move
> (run, walk, jump)

### 4. Poetry

Have students write the letters of their names vertically on a sheet of paper. Then have them use each letter to begin a line of a poem. Have them tell about themselves. Here is an example:

> **L**ikes to read
> **I**s funny sometimes
> **Z**ips through chocolate cake

### 5. Comparisons

Have students compare themselves with their parents. Have them tell how they are alike and how they are different. Then have them compare two classrooms, two teachers, two games, two pets, two hobbies, two friends, and so on.

### 6. Crossword Puzzles

Have students write down interesting words from a story or book and define the terms in the context of the story. Then have them use the words to make a crossword puzzle. Here is an example:

> Henry = main character
> ran = how he got home

|   | H |   |   |
|---|---|---|---|
|   | E |   |   |
|   | N |   |   |
| R | A | N |   |
|   | Y |   |   |

### 7. Word Associations

Have students write a list of words associated with a given topic. Then have them read their words aloud. Discuss how the words are related. Here is an example:

> Winter—cold, snow, ice, snowman, snowballs, snowsuits, sweaters, mittens, scarves, hats, sleds, hills

### 8. Add-Ons

Name an object and direct the students to draw a picture of it. Continue to name additional objects for the students to draw. Here is an example:

> "Draw a picture of a house with a chimney. Now add two more windows, three trees, and another chimney. Put a sidewalk in front."

### 9. Blobs

Ask students to think of a word and write three sentences using it. Then have them read their sentences aloud, substituting the word *blob* for the word. Have other students try to guess what the original word is. Here is an example:

> The *blob* shone in the sky.
> There was a full *blob* last night.
> We danced by the light of the *blob*.

### 10. Scrambled Sentences

Write the words of a sentence in scrambled order. Have students race to unscramble them. Then, have them scramble their own sentences for each other to unscramble.

### 11. Semantic Mapping

Have students make a diagram with a superordinate word in the center circle, as indicated below. Then have them fill in the rest of the diagram. This activity is useful for prereading, reading, and postreading.

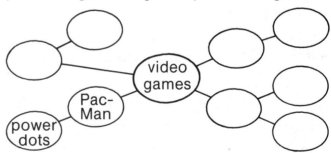

### 12. Sentence Development

Have students write sentences according to a pattern. Here is an example:

> *who + did what + how + where + when*
>
> Felicia watched a movie happily at home last night.

## 13. Naming and Listing
Have students make lists, verbal or written, on topics such as the following:

items that are sharp
names of fish
towns in your state
things that are red

## 14. Reminiscences
Have the students tell about past experiences, using such topics as the following:
My Worst Punishment
My First Bus Ride
My Best Birthday
My Hobby

## 15. Sequential Stories
Have one student write the first sentence of a story. Then have other students add one sentence each. Finally, read the story aloud and discuss how stories can be written.

## 16. Emotional Words
Have students read a passage and ask them to describe their own emotions as they read. Then have them answer the following questions:

Would you want to live next door to the main character?

Why do you think as you do?

How does the author feel about an event or character?

How do you know?

Have students look for words that indicate feelings and either list or underline them.

## 17. Menus
Have students write a menu with a specific purpose. Here are some examples:

lunch for vegetarians
dinner at a dairy-food restaurant
a picnic for four people

## 18. Name the Ways
Ask students a question that requires a list of words as an answer. Divide class into teams and have each team try to come up with the greatest number of possibilities. Here are some examples:

In what ways can a horse move? (gallop, trot, walk, canter, prance, and so on)

How does wood feel? (smooth, splintery, wet, dry, rough, bumpy, and so on)

## 19. Thank You!
Have students group adjectives under the headings "Thank you!" and "No, thank you!" according to whether or not the adjectives are complimentary. Here are some examples:

| *Thank you!* | *No, thank you!* |
|---|---|
| friendly | silly |
| helpful | selfish |
| hardworking | pushy |

## 20. Picture Vocabulary
Draw the outline of a figure, name it, and then have students fill it with descriptive words. Here are some examples:

*My Teacher*

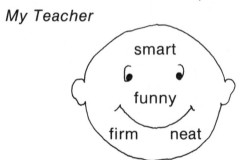

*My House*

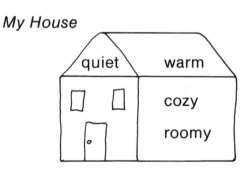

**Name** _____

Put an X on the line if the two words
mean almost the same thing.

1. fat     wide     _____

2. rabbit     bunny     _____

3. sad     happy     _____

4. chair     seat     _____

5. tall     short     _____

6. fast     slow     _____

7. speedy     quick     _____

8. could     didn't     _____

9. might     may     _____     17. cake     pig     _____

10. often     never     _____     18. cow     calf     _____

11. feet     shoe     _____     19. cat     kitten     _____

12. strong     weak     _____     20. rug     carpet     _____

13. icy     cold     _____     21. new     used     _____

14. smart     clever     _____     22. note     letter     _____

15. nice     ugly     _____     23. wood     saw     _____

16. bus     dog     _____     24. fire     flame     _____

*Main Idea Maneuvers*, © 1986 David S. Lake Publishers

◯ = too easy     ▢ = too hard     △ = just right

**7**

**Skill:** Identifying repetition and redundancy

**Name** _____

Put an X on the line if the two words mean almost the same thing.

1. rock     stone     _____

2. shop     store     _____

3. boat     ship     _____

4. jump     swim     _____

5. sock     sack     _____

6. lot     little     _____

7. bag     sack     _____

8. sick     ill     _____

9. job     work     _____     17. smile     grin     _____

10. cup     mug     _____     18. glue     paste     _____

11. gift     present     _____     19. throw     toss     _____

12. pants     slacks     _____     20. sea     ocean     _____

13. mile     inch     _____     21. penny     coin     _____

14. walk     hike     _____     22. bloom     blossom     _____

15. cook     bake     _____     23. wash     clean     _____

16. shovel     dime     _____     24. cold     chilly     _____

 **8**    ◯ = too easy     ▢ = too hard     △ = just right

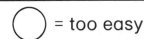

**Skill:** Identifying repetition and redundancy

*Main Idea Maneuvers,* © 1986 David S. Lake Publishers

**Name** _____

Put an X on the line if the two sentences mean almost the same thing.

1. My mom likes pizza.

   My mom enjoys pizza. _____

2. I am seven years old.

   I have had seven birthdays. _____

3. Jan is the best runner.

   The winner of the race is Jan. _____

4. The big dog took a nap.

   The large dog ate some meat. _____

5. The ground was wet after the rain.

   The rain made the ground damp. _____

6. This story is not true.

   I like this story. _____

7. What is in the box?

   I want the gift now. _____

8. There is cake left on the plate.

   Some cake is still on the plate. _____

*Main Idea Maneuvers,* © 1986 David S. Lake Publishers

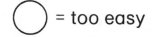 = too easy     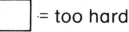 = too hard     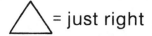 = just right

**Skill:** Identifying repetition and redundancy

**Name** _____

Put an X on the line if the two sentences mean almost the same thing.

1. I need a drink.

   I am thirsty. _____

2. Summer is very hot.

   It is hot in the summertime. _____

3. Tickets are not free.

   Tickets cost money. _____

4. Carla has a sore foot.

   Carla's foot is painful. _____

5. Push the door to go in.

   Open the door by pulling it. _____

6. I sleep in the upper bunk.

   My bunk is on top. _____

7. Look at the dog shake his tail!

   See that dog wag his tail! _____

8. The baby is getting sleepy.

   The baby is not drowsy. _____

**10**

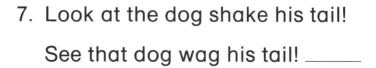 = too easy   = too hard   = just right

**Skill:** Identifying repetition and redundancy

*Main Idea Maneuvers,* © 1986 David S. Lake Publishers

**Name** _____

Put an X by the word that means almost the same as the underlined word.

1. The boy was <u>weeping</u>.    cleaning _____    crying _____

2. Sue <u>liked</u> ice cream.    enjoyed _____    disliked _____

3. My hat is made of <u>cloth</u>.    wool _____    metal _____

4. You need a <u>sharp</u> pencil.    stale _____    pointed _____

5. Don't fall into the <u>pit</u>.    water _____    hole _____

6. I like to <u>wash</u> the table.    clean _____    set _____

7. Mike plays soccer <u>often</u>.    never _____    daily _____

8. Lisa walked on the <u>path</u> in the woods.    trail _____    grass _____

9. You <u>may</u> see Mickey Mouse.    will _____    might _____

10. Some clever boys <u>fixed</u> the bike.    repaired _____    painted _____

11. The grass is <u>damp</u> today.    wet _____    green _____

12. Our <u>plane</u> leaves at noon.    bus _____    jet _____

*Main Idea Maneuvers,* © 1986 David S. Lake Publishers

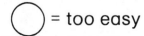 ◯ = too easy     ▢ = too hard     △ = just right

**11**

**Skill:** Identifying repetition and redundancy

**Name** _____

Next to each word, write another word
that has almost the same meaning.

1. happy    _____

2. rabbit    _____

3. quick    _____

4. mother    _____

5. warm    _____

6. big    _____

7. speedy    _____

8. sleepy    _____

9. cap    _____

10. pond    _____

11. nap    _____

12. breeze    _____

13. paste    _____

14. say    _____

15. road    _____

16. sound    _____

17. good    _____

18. bad    _____

19. look    _____

20. scream    _____

21. cord    _____

22. trash    _____

**12**

**Skill:** Identifying repetition and redundancy

*Main Idea Maneuvers,* © 1986 David S. Lake Publishers

**Name** _____

1. Underline the words that tell **the dog was not small.**

   The big dog barked as Debbie walked by. He was so large that he looked like a wolf. Debbie thought the dog was the biggest animal she had ever seen.

2. Underline the words that tell **Bill went home fast.**

   Bill ran home from school. He wanted to play with his new ball. He hurried along. When Bill got home, he was tired because he had run all the way.

3. Underline the words that tell **I like to play.**

   I enjoy playing with small cars. I have fun with jump ropes, too. My best times are when my friends and I are playing.

4. Underline the words that tell **Ann was sick.**

   Ann did not feel well. She wanted to go to bed. Ann's head hurt and she felt sick. Her mother said she was ill.

*Main Idea Maneuvers,* © 1986 David S. Lake Publishers

◯ = too easy  ▢ = too hard  △ = just right

**13**

**Skill:** Identifying repetition and redundancy

1. Underline the words that tell **it was dark.**

   With only a few stars shining, the sky was dark. The sun was gone and there was no light. It was hard to see in the blackness.

2. Underline the words that tell **how Bruce feels about eating.**

   Bruce likes to eat. He enjoys lunch and looks forward to dinner. Snacks are nice for him, too.

3. Underline the words that tell **Celeste was not weak.**

   Celeste was very strong. She used her big muscles to carry things. Her friends said she was tough.

4. Underline the words that tell **my home and school are close.**

   My home is near the school. I live close to the playground. When I walk home from school, I do not walk far.

**14**   ⬭ = too easy   ▢ = too hard   △ = just right

**Skill:** Identifying repetition and redundancy

*Main Idea Maneuvers,* © 1986 David S. Lake Publishers

**Name** _____

Circle the word that does not fit.

1. nose     leg     eyes     ears

2. late     before     then     happy

3. over     near     under     what

4. tree     green     plant     bush

5. rock     stone     shell     pebble

6. rain     flood     water     thunder

7. beak     claw     feather     wind

8. sad     unhappy     mad     glad

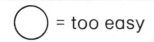 = too easy     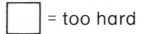 = too hard     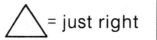 = just right

**15**

**Skill:** Determining relevance

**Name** _____

Circle the word that does not fit.

1. bed        book        table        chair

2. dog        cat         horse        state

3. mine       his         yours        play

4. run        jump        rope         hop

5. cup        cow         plate        dish

6. swim       paint       draw         color

7. bee        honey       fly          wasp

8. flat       smooth      bumpy        red

**16**

 = too easy     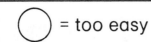 = too hard     △ = just right

**Skill:** Determining relevance

*Main Idea Maneuvers*, © 1986 David S. Lake Publishers

**Name** _____

Draw a different picture in each box to
show what the word means.

1. pets

2. home

3. school

4. fast

◯ = too easy    ▢ = too hard    △ = just right

**17**

**Skill:** Determining relevance

**Name** _____

Draw a different picture in each box to show what the word means.

1. zoo

2. food

3. toys

4. people

**18**

○ = too easy     □ = too hard     △ = just right

**Skill:** Determining relevance

**Name** _____

Write two words that belong in each group.

1.  things you can eat _____ _____

2.  things you can wear _____ _____

3.  things that have wings _____ _____

4.  things that are red _____ _____

5.  foods that are sweet _____ _____

6.  things that are wet _____ _____

7.  toys that have wheels _____ _____

8.  kinds of pets _____ _____

9.  kinds of jobs _____ _____

10. things in the sky _____ _____

11. things used for play _____ _____

12. places to work _____ _____

*Main Idea Maneuvers,* © 1986 David S. Lake Publishers

◯ = too easy   ☐ = too hard   △ = just right

**19**

**Skill:** Determining relevance

**Name** _____

Underline the words that tell **how.**

1. The man left in a hurry.

2. Pat shook her head sadly.

3. Slowly, the flag went up.

4. Joe smiled happily when he won.

5. The camper stood bravely near the bear.

6. Suddenly, the lights went out.

7. Luckily, we found a place to buy gas.

8. Kelly talked loudly in the library.

**20**

| ◯ = too easy | ▢ = too hard | △ = just right |
| --- | --- | --- |

**Skill:** Determining relevance

*Main Idea Maneuvers,* © 1986 David S. Lake Publishers

**Name** _____

Underline the words that tell **when.**

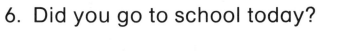

1. We worked hard all day.

2. The man will run faster next time.

3. In a few days, we will play ball.

4. Last summer, I went to the beach.

5. You may wash your hands before you eat.

6. Did you go to school today?

7. My mother works hard every day.

8. We see many flowers in May.

◯ = too easy     ▢ = too hard     △ = just right

**21**

**Skill:** Determining relevance

**Name** _____

Underline the words that tell **where.**

1.  We went into the water to cool off.

2.  The bird sang near the top of the tree.

3.  Put the paper under the book.

4.  Over the table was a fine cloth.

5.  We ate lunch at the old rest stop.

6.  How does Don drive down the road?

7.  A large rock is in your path.

8.  Feed the animals beside the cage.

**22**

**Skill:** Determining relevance

Main Idea Maneuvers, © 1986 David S. Lake Publishers

**Name** _____

Underline the words that tell **who.**

1. The first people came to school early.

2. Are those toys for Andy and me?

3. Ben Franklin was born in 1706.

4. The books were read by first-graders.

5. Lucy wanted to go home.

6. Let everybody play on the swings.

7. They left the party early.

8. My older sister likes to travel.

Who is this?

◯ = too easy    ▢ = too hard    △ = just right

**23**

**Skill:** Determining relevance

**Name** _____

Draw a different picture in each box to show what the words mean.

1. things in the sky

2. things you can ride

3. things used for cooking

4. people who work

**24**

◯ = too easy     ▢ = too hard     △ = just right

**Skill:** Classifying nouns

**Name** _____

Draw a different picture in each box to show what the words mean.

1. kinds of clothing

2. types of shoes

3. things that make music

4. tools for building

◯ = too easy     ▢ = too hard     △ = just right

# 25

**Skill:** Classifying nouns

**Name** _____

Tell how the words belong together.

1. wagon
   truck
   bus _____

2. racket
   ball
   net _____

3. hammer
   saw
   nail _____

4. flashlight
   lantern
   lamp _____

5. cat
   bird
   dog _____

6. spoon
   plate
   bowl _____

7. cookies
   candy
   cake _____

8. brush
   hairpin
   comb _____

# 26

| ◯ = too easy | ▢ = too hard | △ = just right |

**Skill:** Classifying nouns

*Main Idea Maneuvers*, © 1986 David S. Lake Publishers

**Name** _____

Tell how the words belong together.

1. raincoat
   umbrella
   boots _____

2. banana
   orange
   apple _____

3. sleeping bag
   tent
   cot _____

4. cheese
   ice cream
   milk _____

5. crayon
   chalk
   pen _____

6. window
   door
   roof _____

7. shampoo
   toothpaste
   soap _____

8. Mary
   Susan
   Sara _____

*Main Idea Maneuvers*, © 1986 David S. Lake Publishers

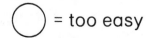 = too easy   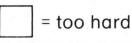 = too hard   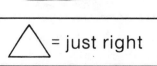 = just right

**27**

**Skill:** Classifying nouns

**Name** _____

List three things that show what the
word or words mean.

1. names of boys

_____

_____

_____

2. colors

_____

_____

_____

3. things to read

_____

_____

_____

4. animals

_____

_____

_____

5. picnic things

_____

_____

_____

6. tools

_____

_____

_____

7. things found in the water

_____

_____

_____

8. flowers

_____

_____

_____

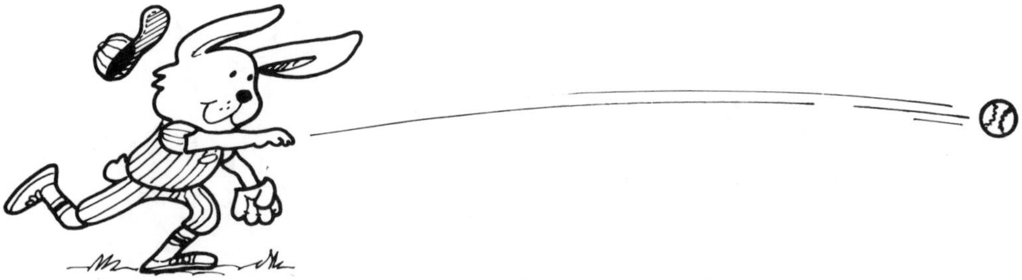

# 28

| ◯ = too easy | ▢ = too hard | △ = just right |

**Skill:** Classifying nouns

*Main Idea Maneuvers,* © 1986 David S. Lake Publishers

**Name** _____

List three things that show what the
word or words mean.

1. fruit

_____

_____

_____

2. items used for carrying

_____

_____

_____

3. food for breakfast

_____

_____

_____

4. items in the hospital

_____

_____

_____

5. baby things

_____

_____

_____

6. things used for cleaning

_____

_____

_____

7. things on the playground

_____

_____

_____

8. things that are not safe

_____

_____

_____

*Main Idea Maneuvers,* © 1986 David S. Lake Publishers

◯ = too easy        ▢ = too hard        △ = just right

**29**

**Skill:** Classifying nouns

**Name** _____

For each sentence, underline the words that form a list. Tell how the words belong together.

1. A doctor, a nurse, and a dentist rushed in.

   _____

2. My father needs a mop, a sponge, and a cloth now.

   _____

3. Let's take Paul, Sid, and Tom to the movies.

   _____

4. We saw hats, horns, and a cake at the party.

   _____

5. The zoo was full of lions, bears, and monkeys.

   _____

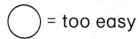
**30**

| ◯ = too easy | ▢ = too hard | △ = just right |
| --- | --- | --- |

**Skill:** Classifying nouns

**Name** _____

For each sentence, underline the words that form a list. Tell how the words belong together.

1. In the morning we eat bread, fruit, and cereal.

_____

2. You need to bring a coat, a hat, and boots.

_____

3. Betty, Joan, and Marie went home.

_____

4. Chris used forks, spoons, and knives.

_____

5. When will the letters, cards, and papers come?

_____

**31**

*Main Idea Maneuvers*, © 1986 David S. Lake Publishers

**Skill:** Classifying nouns

**Name** _____

Draw a different picture in each box to
show what the words mean.

1. playing
   in the snow

2. getting
   clean

3. camping
   in the
   woods

4. getting
   ready for
   school

**32**

◯ = too easy          ▢ = too hard          △ = just right

**Skill:** Classifying series of events

*Main Idea Maneuvers,* © 1986 David S. Lake Publishers

**Name** _____

Draw a different picture in each box to show what the words mean.

1. fixing your hair

2. giving a present

3. finding a coin

4. winning a race

◯ = too easy     ▢ = too hard     △ = just right

**33**

*Main Idea Maneuvers*, © 1986 David S. Lake Publishers

**Skill:** Classifying series of events

**Name** _____

Tell what is happening.

1. kicking
   hopping
   stamping

   _____

   _____

2. baking
   roasting
   frying

   _____

   _____

3. cutting
   pasting
   coloring

   _____

   _____

4. counting
   adding
   subtracting

   _____

   _____

5. napping
   snoring
   dreaming

   _____

   _____

**34** $\bigcirc$ = too easy   $\square$ = too hard   $\triangle$ = just right

**Skill:** Classifying series of events

*Main Idea Maneuvers,* © 1986 David S. Lake Publishers

**Name** _____

Tell what is happening.

1. running
   falling
   crying

   _____

   _____

2. hammering
   sawing
   measuring

   _____

   _____

3. yelling
   singing
   talking

   _____

   _____

4. waving
   clapping
   pointing

   _____

   _____

5. biting
   chewing
   swallowing

   _____

   _____

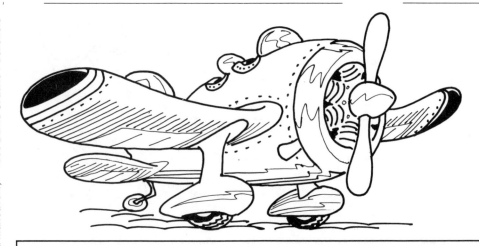

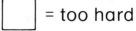 = too easy    ☐ = too hard    △ = just right

**35**

**Skill:** Classifying series of events

*Main Idea Maneuvers,* © 1986 David S. Lake Publishers

**Name** _____

List three steps for each activity below.

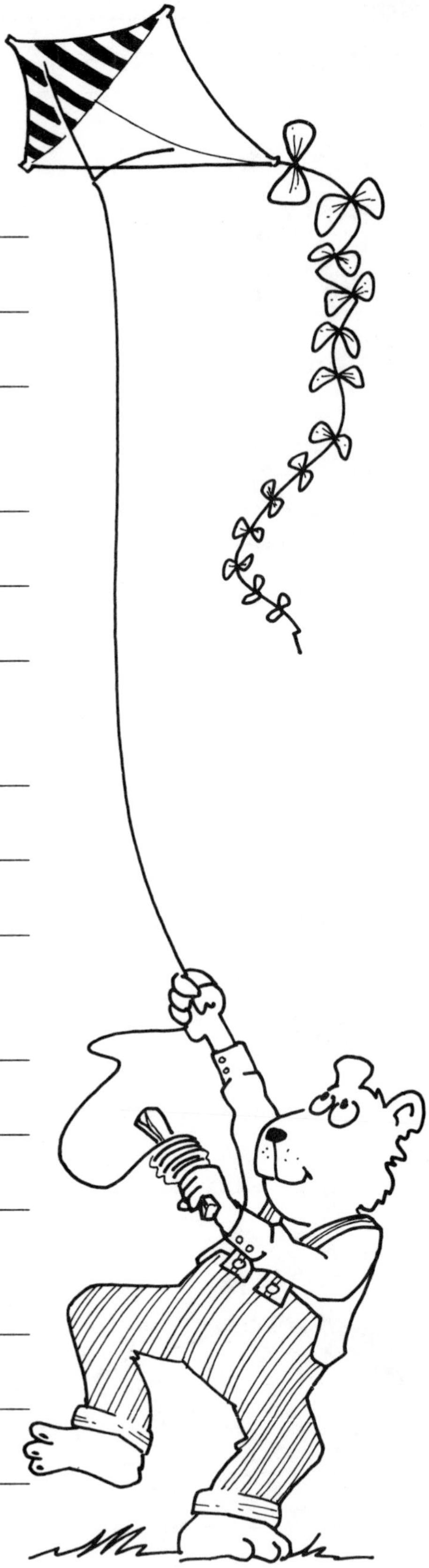

1. flying a kite

_____

_____

_____

2. digging a hole

_____

_____

_____

3. taking a picture

_____

_____

_____

4. eating lunch

_____

_____

_____

5. having a party

_____

_____

_____

# 36

◯ = too easy   ☐ = too hard   △ = just right

**Skill:** Classifying series of events

Main Idea Maneuvers, © 1986 David S. Lake Publishers

List three steps for each activity below.

1. taking a trip

   _____

   _____

   _____

2. making cookies

   _____

   _____

   _____

3. going to school

   _____

   _____

   _____

4. going swimming

   _____

   _____

   _____

5. building a house

   _____

   _____

   _____

*Main Idea Maneuvers*, © 1986 David S. Lake Publishers

◯ = too easy        ▢ = too hard        △ = just right

**37**

**Skill:** Classifying series of events

**Name** _____

Underline the series of events. Tell what
the sentence is about.

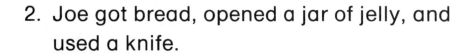

1. The baby stood up, took a step, and fell
   down.

   _____

2. Joe got bread, opened a jar of jelly, and
   used a knife.

   _____

3. Our team had the ball, ran fast, and won the
   game.

   _____

4. The dog sat up, barked, and took the treat.

   _____

5. Sandy opened the lunch box, unwrapped the sandwich, and took
   a bite.

   _____

**38** ⬤ = too easy ▢ = too hard △ = just right

**Skill:** Classifying series of events

*Main Idea Maneuvers,* © 1986 David S. Lake Publishers

**Name** _____

Underline the series of events. Tell what
the sentence is about.

1. The gun went off, the boys ran, and the fans
cheered.

_____

2. Rain came down, the streets flooded, and
things were washed away.

_____

3. The fire fighters came quickly, used big
hoses, and put the fire out.

_____

4. I opened the book, read slowly, and looked at the pictures.

_____

5. We gave the woman money, took our bag, and left the store.

_____

○ = too easy    □ = too hard    △ = just right    **39**

**Skill:** Classifying series of events

**Name** _____

Copy the sentence that tells what each passage is about.

1. Try to be nice to other people. Help them when you can. Don't say mean things.

   _____

   _____

2. We like to eat fish. We also like cake. We like many kinds of food.

   _____

   _____

3. Last night the sky was dark. There was a scary sound. I was afraid last night!

   _____

   _____

4. Cookies are easy to make. First, put flour and sugar together. Add butter. Then, bake the cookies.

   _____

   _____

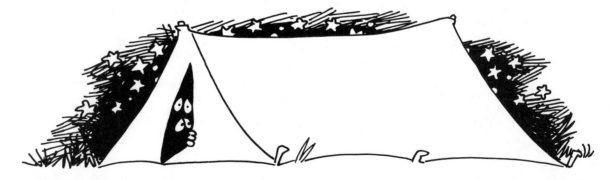

**40**  ◯ = too easy    ▢ = too hard    △ = just right

**Skill:** Identifying topic sentences

Main Idea Maneuvers, © 1986 David S. Lake Publishers

**Name** _____

Copy the sentence that tells what each
passage is about.

1. I play with my cat. First, I throw a small ball. My cat runs after it.
Then, I pull the ball away from the cat's claws.

_____

_____

2. Some people are very strong. They can lift heavy things. Their
muscles are big. These people can move heavy objects.

_____

_____

3. The flowers looked nice. We picked them and put them in a vase.
We had red ones and yellow ones.

_____

_____

4. Jenny opened the candy jar carefully. She took one piece out.
She chewed slowly. Jenny enjoyed the candy.

_____

_____

| ◯ = too easy | ▢ = too hard | △ = just right | **41** |

**Name** _____

Copy the sentence that tells what each passage is about.

1.  Newspapers tell about the world. They tell about what happens each day. Newspapers also tell what will happen soon.

    _____

    _____

2.  My brother made lunch today. He smiled when he gave me some soup and a sandwich. He made the same things for himself.

    _____

    _____

3.  Henry's bird died. The bird was old and sick. Henry loved his bird. He cried when it died.

    _____

    _____

4.  I like to swim. You like to play in the sand. We like to walk by the water. We enjoy the beach!

    _____

    _____

# 42

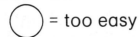 = too easy      ☐ = too hard      △ = just right

**Skill:** Identifying topic sentences

Main Idea Maneuvers, © 1986 David S. Lake Publishers

**Name** _____

Copy the sentence that tells what each passage is about.

1. My new dress is too short. It is hard to put on. It looks funny. My new dress does not fit.

_____

_____

2. My friend works hard. She drives a tractor. She takes care of animals. She plants a big garden.

_____

_____

3. Buy a zinky toy! You will have fun with it. Lots of boys and girls have one. Zinky toys do not cost much.

_____

_____

4. The last time I drank a soda was in the summer. It was a hot day. I hoped the soda would cool me off.

_____

_____

 = too easy     ☐ = too hard     △ = just right     **43**

**Skill:** Identifying topic sentences

**Name** _____

Draw a picture in each box. Under each
box write one sentence to tell about
your picture.

1. _____

_____

2. _____

_____

**44**

○ = too easy     □ = too hard     △ = just right

**Skill:** Inventing topic sentences

*Main Idea Maneuvers,* © 1986 David S. Lake Publishers

**Name** _____

For each group of words, write a
sentence to tell how the words belong
together.

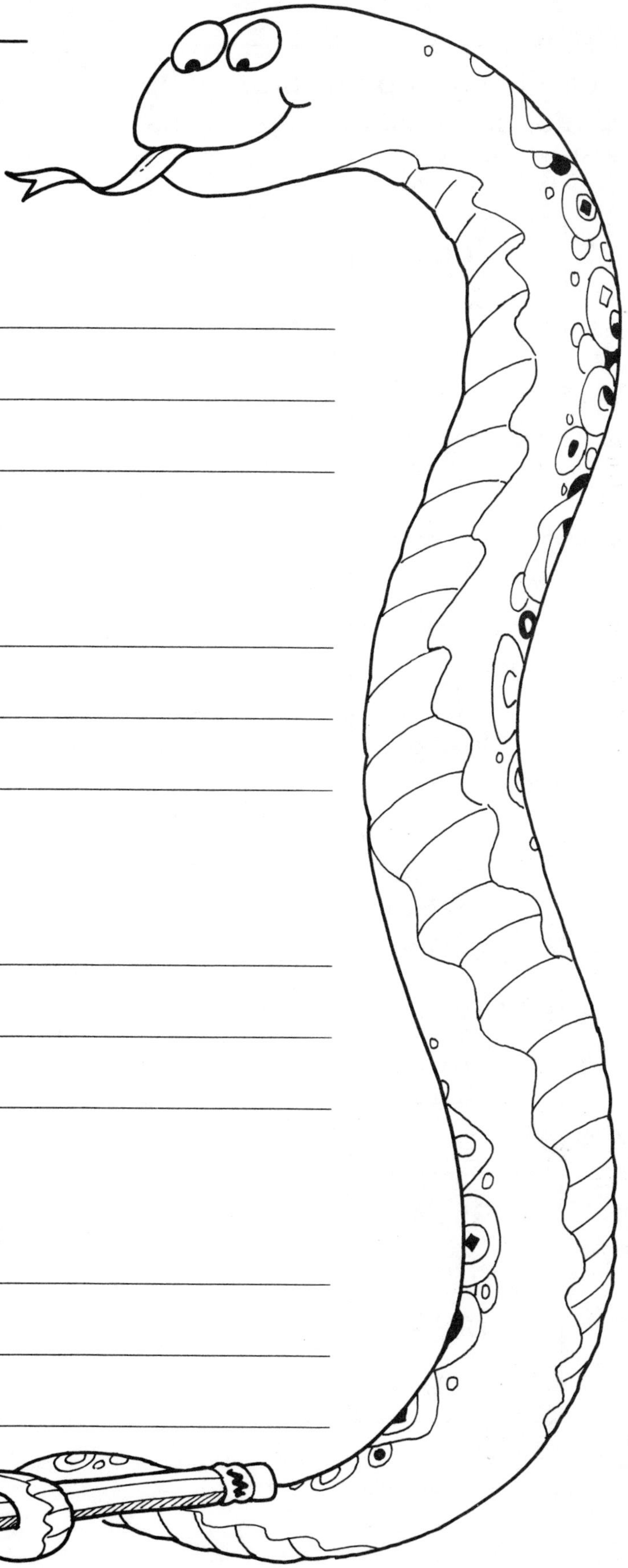

1.
| hat |
| coat |
| pants |
| shoes |

_____
_____
_____

2.
| happy |
| glad |
| smile |
| enjoy |

_____
_____
_____

3.
| fire |
| burn |
| hot |
| heat |

_____
_____
_____

4.
| late |
| last |
| behind |
| end |

_____
_____
_____

◯ = too easy     ▢ = too hard     △ = just right

# 45

**Skill:** Inventing topic sentences

**Name** _____

For each group of words, write a
sentence to tell how the words
belong together.

1.
| ice |
| snow |
| frost |
| ice cream |

_____
_____
_____

2.
| run |
| jump |
| play |
| swing |

_____
_____
_____

3.
| red |
| yellow |
| green |
| blue |

_____
_____
_____

4.
| throw |
| hit |
| ball |
| mitt |

_____
_____
_____

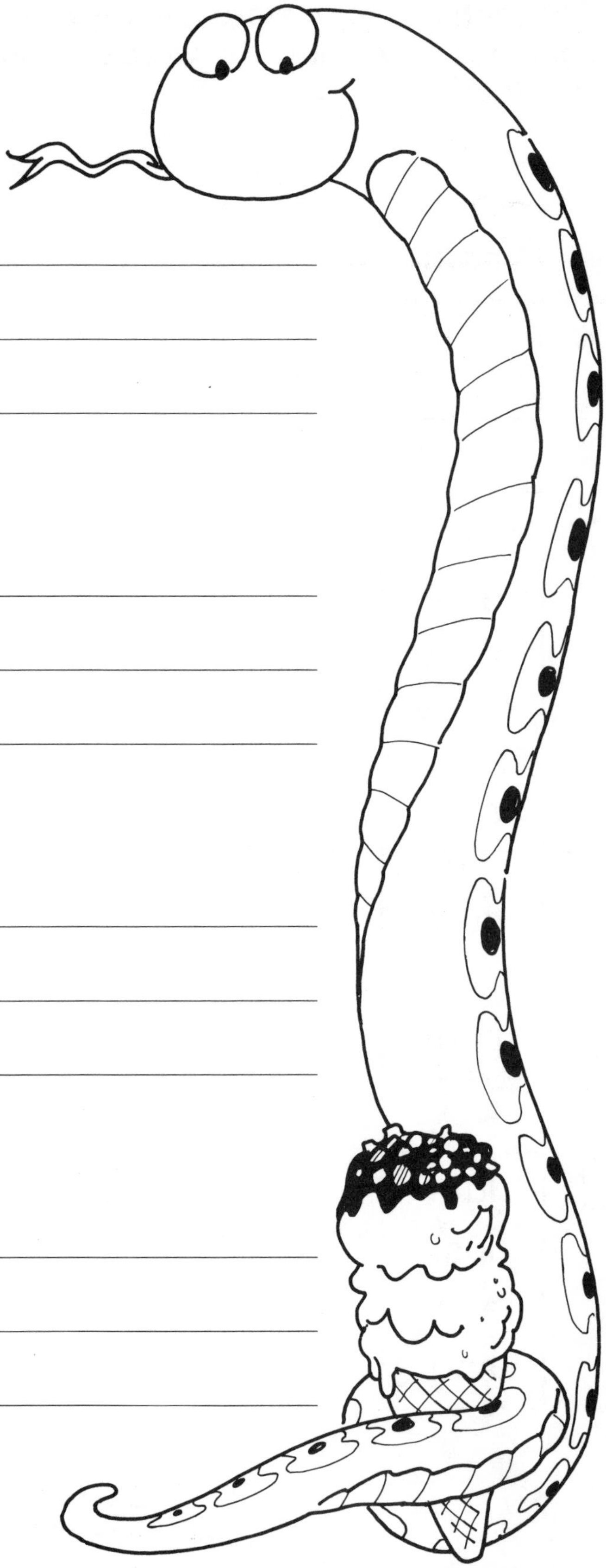

**46**

◯ = too easy        ▢ = too hard        △ = just right

**Skill:** Inventing topic sentences

*Main Idea Maneuvers,* © 1986 David S. Lake Publishers

**Name** _____

Write a new sentence to tell what each passage is about.

1. Jim packed a bag. He put in socks, pants, shirts, and one toothbrush. Jim took the bag with him when he left the house.

_____

_____

2. The baby was crying. Dad gave the baby some food. Then he held her close for a while. The baby went to sleep.

_____

_____

3. Boys and girls came out of the classroom. They ran to the playground. Some children went over to the swings.

_____

_____

4. That is a pretty box. Is it a gift? Is it something that is alive? I want to know what is in that box.

_____

_____

◯ = too easy      ▢ = too hard      △ = just right

**47** ✓

**Skill:** Inventing topic sentences

**Name** _____

Underline the answer that best tells
about each group of words.

1.
| rabbit |
| fox |
| squirrel |

  a. animal pets
  b. animals in the woods
  c. my pets

2.
| can |
| box |
| bag |

  a. things used for cooking
  b. things to hold other things
  c. toys for children

3.
| wagon |
| ball |
| bike |

  a. toys with wheels
  b. toys for babies
  c. outside toys

4.
| banana |
| orange |
| apple |

  a. food for lunch
  b. fruit
  c. food I like

5.
| blanket |
| pillow |
| sheet |

  a. warm things
  b. things to take on a trip
  c. bed things

**48**

◯ = too easy     ▢ = too hard     △ = just right

**Skill:** Identifying main idea

Main Idea Maneuvers, © 1986 David S. Lake Publishers

**Name** _____

Underline the answer that best tells
about each group of words.

1.
| gallop |
| trot |
| run |

a. things that make music
b. ways a horse moves
c. kinds of dancing

2.
| beside |
| near |
| close |

a. under
b. over
c. nearby

3.
| bad |
| evil |
| wicked |

a. kind
b. nice
c. not good

4.
| rushed |
| ran |
| hurried |

a. went quickly
b. wanted to play
c. went home

5.
| napping |
| dozing |
| sleeping |

a. being quiet
b. moving slowly
c. taking a rest

 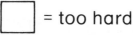

**Name** _____

Underline the answer that best tells about each group of words.

1.
| elephant |
| tiger |
| monkey |

  a. wild animals
  b. pets
  c. animals that fly

2.
| jelly |
| jam |
| honey |

  a. food we like
  b. food with salt
  c. food that is sweet

3.
| cry |
| frown |
| weep |

  a. being glad
  b. being silly
  c. being sad

4.
| said |
| asked |
| told |

  a. Someone spoke.
  b. He was told.
  c. We want to know.

5.
| dig |
| plow |
| hoe |

  a. working inside
  b. working in dirt
  c. playing at school

**50**

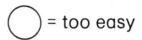 = too easy    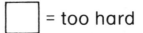 = too hard    △ = just right

**Skill:** Identifying main idea

Main Idea Maneuvers, © 1986 David S. Lake Publishers

**Name** _____

Underline the answer that best tells about each group of words.

1.
| green |
| red |
| purple |

a. names of colors
b. paints
c. crayons

2.
| paper |
| pencil |
| eraser |

a. a nice present
b. writing things
c. coloring things

3.
| she |
| her |
| Miss |

a. words about my friend
b. short words
c. words about a woman

4.
| first |
| next |
| later |

a. words that tell when
b. words that tell who
c. spelling words

5.
| smiling |
| happy |
| glad |

a. not pretty
b. not sad
c. not good

⭕ = too easy    ⬜ = too hard    △ = just right

**51**

**Skill:** Identifying main idea

**Name** _____

Draw a picture to show each idea. Put
at least four things in each picture.

1. having a party

2. going swimming

3. taking care of animals

**52**

⬭ = too easy　　▢ = too hard　　△ = just right

**Skill:** Identifying main idea

*Main Idea Maneuvers,* © 1986 David S. Lake Publishers

**Name** _____

Draw a picture to show each idea. Put
at least four things in each picture.

1. helping at
   home

2. traveling

3. being happy

**53**

**Skill:** Identifying main idea

**Name** _____

Draw a picture to show each idea. Put at least four things in each picture.

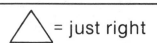

1. a circus

2. something scary

3. my best friend

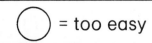

**54**

◯ = too easy    ▢ = too hard    △ = just right

*Main Idea Maneuvers,* © 1986 David S. Lake Publishers

Make up a title for each of these things.

1. your best place to play

    _____

    _____

2. a refrigerator

    _____

    _____

3. a book about you

    _____

    _____

4. a story about your school

    _____

5. a magazine for children

    _____

6. your best toy

    _____

| ◯ = too easy | ▢ = too hard | △ = just right | **55** |

**Skill:** Understanding and using titles

**Name** _____

Make up a title for each of these things.

1. a cookbook for food to go in
   lunch boxes

   _____

   _____

2. a special day at the zoo

   _____

   _____

3. a television show

   _____

   _____

4. a breakfast food

   _____

5. a book about living on the moon

   _____

6. a scary story

   _____

◯ = too easy    ☐ = too hard    △ = just right

**Skill:** Understanding and using titles

*Main Idea Maneuvers,* © 1986 David S. Lake Publishers

**Name** _____

Write three sentences about each book.

**Best Friends**

1. _____
_____
_____
_____
_____
_____

**Ouch!**

2. _____
_____
_____
_____
_____
_____

**Do Not Touch**

3. _____
_____
_____
_____
_____
_____

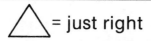

◯ = too easy      ▢ = too hard      △ = just right

**57**

**Skill:** Understanding and using titles

**Name** _____

Write three sentences about each book.

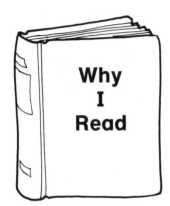

**Why I Read**

I. _____

_____

_____

_____

_____

_____

**All About Me**

2. _____

_____

_____

_____

_____

_____

**Jokes**

3. _____

_____

_____

_____

_____

_____

**58**

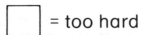 = too easy   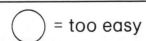 = too hard   △ = just right

**Skill:** Understanding and using titles

*Main Idea Maneuvers*, © 1986 David S. Lake Publishers

# Answer Key

**Page 7**
The following pairs of words should have an X on the line:
1, 2, 4, 7, 9, 13, 14, 18, 19, 20, 22, and 24.

**Page 8**
The following pairs of words should have an X on the line:
1, 2, 3, 7, 8, 9, 10, 11, 12, 14, 15, 17, 18, 19, 20, 21, 22, 23, and 24.

**Page 9**
The following pairs of sentences should have an X on the line:
1, 2, 3, 5, and 8.

**Page 10**
The following pairs of sentences should have an X on the line:
1, 2, 3, 4, 6, and 7.

**Page 11**
The following words should have an X on the line:
1. crying, 2. enjoyed, 3. wool, 4. pointed, 5. hole, 6. clean, 7. daily, 8. trail, 9. might, 10. repaired, 11. wet, 12. jet.

**Page 12**
Accept a synonym for each word.

**Page 13**
The following words should be underlined (accept some variation):
1. big, large, wolf, biggest; 2. ran, hurried, had run; 3. enjoy playing, have fun, best times; 4. did not feel well, wanted to go to bed, head hurt, felt sick, was ill.

**Page 14**
The following words should be underlined (accept some variation):
1. sky was dark, sun was gone, no light, hard to see, blackness; 2. likes to eat, enjoys lunch, looks forward to dinner, Snacks are nice; 3. very strong, big muscles, tough; 4. near, close, do not walk far.

**Page 15**
The following words should be circled:
1. leg, 2. happy, 3. what, 4. green, 5. shell, 6. thunder, 7. wind, 8. glad.

## Page 16
The following words should be circled:
1. book, 2. state, 3. play, 4. rope, 5. cow, 6. swim, 7. honey, 8. red.

## Page 17
Accept appropriate pictures.

## Page 18
Accept appropriate pictures.

## Page 19
Accept appropriate nouns.

## Page 20
The following words should be underlined:
1. in a hurry, 2. sadly, 3. Slowly, 4. happily, 5. bravely, 6. Suddenly, 7. Luckily, 8. loudly.

## Page 21
The following words should be underlined:
1. all day, 2. next time, 3. In a few days, 4. Last summer, 5. before you eat, 6. today, 7. every day, 8. in May.

## Page 22
The following words should be underlined:
1. into the water, 2. near the top of the tree, 3. under the book, 4. Over the table, 5. at the old rest stop, 6. down the road, 7. in your path, 8. beside the cage.

## Page 23
The following words should be underlined:
1. The first people, 2. Andy and me, 3. Ben Franklin, 4. first-graders, 5. Lucy, 6. everybody, 7. They, 8. My older sister.

## Page 24
Accept appropriate pictures.

## Page 25
Accept appropriate pictures.

## Page 26
Accept variations of the following answers:
1. things with wheels, 2. things used in tennis, 3. tools, 4. lights, 5. pets, 6. things used for eating, 7. sweet foods, 8. things used for hair.

## Page 27
Accept variations of the following answers:
1. things used in the rain, 2. fruit, 3. things used for camping, 4. dairy foods, 5. writing tools, 6. parts of a building, 7. cleansers, 8. girls' names.

## Page 28
Accept appropriate nouns.

## Page 29
Accept appropriate nouns.

## Page 30
The following words should be underlined and explained (accept some variation in the wording of how the words belong together):
1. doctor, nurse, dentist (people involved with medicine); 2. mop, sponge, cloth (cleaning supplies); 3. Paul, Sid, Tom (boys' names); 4. hats, horns, cake (party things); 5. lions, bears, monkeys (animals).

## Page 31
The following words should be underlined and explained (accept some variation in the wording of how the words belong together):
1. bread, fruit, cereal (breakfast foods); 2. coat, hat, boots (clothing); 3. Betty, Joan, Marie (girls' names); 4. forks, spoons, knives (tools for meals); 5. letters, cards, papers (mail).

## Page 32
Accept appropriate pictures.

*Main Idea Maneuvers*, © 1986 David S. Lake Publishers

**Page 33**

Accept appropriate pictures.

**Page 34**

Accept some variation of the following answers:

1. moving feet, 2. cooking, 3. working on a project (as art), 4. working in arithmetic, 5. sleeping.

**Page 35**

Accept some variation of the following answers:

1. falling down, 2. building something, 3. making sounds, 4. moving hands, 5. eating.

**Page 36**

Accept appropriate answers.

**Page 37**

Accept appropriate answers.

**Page 38**

The following words should be underlined and explained (accept some variation in the wording of what the events are about):

1. stood up, took a step, fell down (learning to walk); 2. got bread, opened a jar of jelly, used a knife (making a snack); 3. had the ball, ran fast, won the game (playing a game); 4. sat up, barked, took the treat (doing a trick); 5. opened the lunch box, unwrapped the sandwich, took a bite (starting lunch).

**Page 39**

The following words should be underlined and explained (accept some variation in the wording of what the events are about):

1. gun went off, boys ran, fans cheered (a race); 2. Rain came down, streets flooded, things were washed away (a rainstorm); 3. fire fighters came quickly, used big hoses, put the fire out (putting out a fire); 4. opened the book, read slowly, looked at the pictures (reading a book); 5. gave the woman money, took our bag, left the store (shopping).

**Page 40**

1. Try to be nice to other people.
2. We like many kinds of food.
3. I was afraid last night!
4. Cookies are easy to make.

**Page 41**

1. I play with my cat.
2. Some people are very strong.
3. The flowers looked nice.
4. Jenny enjoyed the candy.

**Page 42**

1. Newspapers tell about the world.
2. My brother made lunch today.
3. Henry's bird died.
4. We enjoy the beach!

**Page 43**

1. My new dress does not fit.
2. My friend works hard.
3. Buy a zinky toy!
4. The last time I drank a soda was in the summer.

**Page 44**

Accept appropriate pictures and answers.

**Page 45**

Accept appropriate answers.

**Page 46**

Accept appropriate answers.

**Page 47**

Accept appropriate answers.

**Page 48**

The following answers should be underlined:

1. b, 2. b, 3. c, 4. b, 5. c.

**Page 49**

The following answers should be underlined:

1. b, 2. c, 3. c, 4. a, 5. c.

**Page 50**

The following answers should be underlined:

1. a, 2. c, 3. c, 4. a, 5. b.

**Page 51**

The following answers should be underlined:

1. a, 2. b, 3. c, 4. a, 5. b.

**Page 52**

Accept appropriate pictures.

**Page 53**

Accept appropriate pictures.

**Page 54**

Accept appropriate pictures.

**Page 55**

Accept appropriate answers.

**Page 56**

Accept appropriate answers.

**Page 57**

Accept appropriate answers.

**Page 58**

Accept appropriate answers.

*Main Idea Maneuvers*, © 1986 David S. Lake Publishers

Comprehension Capers

# Main Idea Maneuvers

by L. D. Ceaser
Grades 1-3

Help students grasp main ideas in reading with this set of 52 reproducible activities. Each activity provides growth and practice in essential subskills as students progress along the way to mastery of main idea. Each reproducible sheet has a handy evaluation code box so students can evaluate item difficulty. It's a perfect way to keep track of the extra needs of some students while you note the extra strengths of others! Or you can code the items for use with teacher aides and tutors! You and your students will benefit from the content *and* the process provided in this valuable resource. #1475

## MORE COMPREHENSION CAPERS!
Other Evaluation Code Box Reading Activities by L. D. Ceaser

---

## Making Tracks to Main Idea, Grades 4-6

Easy to plan into your reading lesson or supplementary program, these activity sheets focus on essential sub-skills as students learn to read for main ideas. Students will appreciate the opportunity to evaluate their work. #1476

## Making Inferences, Grades 1-3, #1477
## Intent on Inferences, Grades 4-6, #1478

Help students interpret reading material and success-fully make inferences with these easy-to-use activity sheets. As learning increases, reading critically becomes easier and more enjoyable.

For a complete catalog write:

Fearon Teacher Aids
a division of
**David S. Lake Publishers**
19 Davis Drive
Belmont, California 94002

ISBN 0-8224-1475-9